The Great Egg-venture
on Chicken Island

Marcy Schaaf

Welcome to Chicken Island, where the sun always shines, the coconuts are sweet, and the chickens rule the roost! Join us on an egg-citing journey filled with feathers, fun, and a little bit of fowl play. Meet our fearless flock of free-range chickens as they embark on their greatest adventure yet - protecting their precious eggs from the sneaky clutches of Tom, the coconut-craving thief. Get ready to squawk, flap, and laugh along as our feathered friends show us that with a little teamwork and a lot of determination, anything is possible on Chicken Island!

Once upon a squawking time,
on the sunny shores of Chicken
Island...

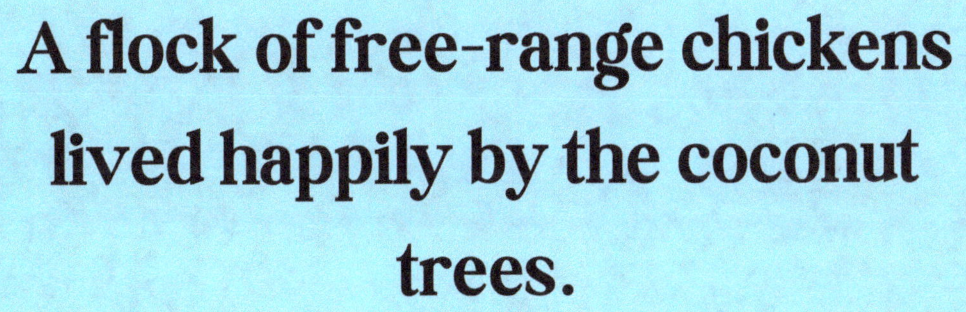

A flock of free-range chickens
lived happily by the coconut
trees.

But one day, they faced a crisis!

Tom, the sneaky thief, wanted their eggs.

"We must protect our eggs!"
clucked Henrietta, the wisest hen.

So, they gathered all their eggs and decided to keep them safe in one big bucket.

Each chicken took turns laying on the eggs while another stood guard.

They built a nest tower,
high enough to spot
Tom coming from afar.

But Tom was clever!
He lured the chickens with
tasty coconut treats.

Free Coconuts

The chickens couldn't resist and

gathered around

Tom's coconut offerings.

The chickens were thrilled and pecked away at the delicious coconut meat.

Meanwhile, Tom eyed the bucket of eggs, planning his next move.

Suddenly,
Henrietta squawked,
"Look out! Tom's after our eggs!"

The chickens hurried back to their nest tower, ready to defend their precious eggs.

Tom approached,
but the chickens were prepared.

Victorious, the chickens
celebrated with a coconut
feast of their own.

From that day on, they kept a close watch on their eggs and their coconut stash.

Tom never dared to mess with the brave and clever chickens of Chicken Island again.

And so, the free-range chickens lived happily ever after, laying eggs and enjoying coconuts under the Hawaiian sun.

The end.

But wait! There's more to cluck about!

Join the chickens on their next
adventure as they explore the
mysteries of Chicken Island.

Will they discover hidden treasures?
Face new challenges? Find out in the
next egg-citing tale!

Thank you for joining us on this feathered adventure. Stay tuned for more fun with the free-range chickens!

And remember, no matter how small
you are, you can always stand tall and
protect what's important to you.

Until next time, keep on clucking
and
cock-a-doodle-dooing!

Psst! Don't forget to share this egg-ceptional story with your friends and family. They'll be egg-static!

Now, go out and spread your wings,
just like our fearless feathered friends.

The end (for real this time).
But the fun never stops on Chicken
Island!

Glossary:

Squawk -

the sound a chicken makes
when it's excited or alarmed.

Feathered Friends -

a term used to describe chickens and other birds.

Egg-citing -
something that is exciting, especially when it involves eggs!

Coconut -

a tropical fruit with a hard shell
and delicious white flesh inside.

Free-range -

chickens that are allowed to roam
freely and enjoy the outdoors.

Mahalo (Thank You) for reading!

The actual chickens this story's about!

The chickens in Hawaii LOVE coconuts!

Books By Schaaf

www.BookBySchaaf.com

Find us at:

www.ingramcontent.com/pod-product-compliance
Lightning Source LLC
Chambersburg PA
CBHW081204130726
47996CB00009B/3234